Nawabi Aloo

Besan Paratha

Zero oil Rotis & Subzis

TARLA DALAL
India's # 1 Cookery Author

S&C
SANJAY & CO.
MUMBAI

Fifth Printing : 2011

ISBN : 978-8-189491-45-1

Price: Rs. 99/-

Published & Distributed by : **Sanjay & Company**

A-1/353, Shah & Nahar Industrial Estate, Dhanraj Mill Compound, Lower Parel (W), Mumbai - 400 013. INDIA.

Tel. : (91-22) 4345 2400 • Fax : (91-22) 2496 5876 • E-mail : sanjay@tarladalal.com • Website : www.tarladalal.com

UK and USA customers can call us on :

UK : 02080029533 • USA : 213-634-1406

For books, Membership on **tarladalal.com**, Subscription for **Cooking & More** and Recipe queries

Timing : Monday to Friday 9.30 a.m. to 6.00 p.m. (IST) and Saturday 9.30 a.m. to 1.30 p.m. (IST)

Local call charges applicable

Recipe Research & Production Design
Arati Fedane
Sanika Chavan-Labhade
Pragnesh Joshi

Nutritionists
Nisha Katira
Sapna Kamdar

Food Styling
Shubhangi Dhaimade

Photography
Jignesh Jhaveri

Typesetting
Adityas Enterprises

Designed by
Satyamangal Rege

Printed by :
Minal Sales Agencies, Mumbai

Copy Editing
Janani Gopalkrishnan

INTRODUCTION

In today's health-conscious world, more and more people are becoming aware of the ill-effects of obesity, and the importance of eating healthy. We often think that eating less and dieting are the best and fastest ways to achieve that perfect hour-glass figure! Although eating less is also important, it is more important to make the right choices of foods and eat them in moderation.

Along with restricting the intake of high-calorie foods, junk foods, sugary foods etc. we also often abstain totally from the consumption of oil and ghee. Although, considered as the biggest culprit of causing weight gain, heart disorders and various other health problems like high blood pressure, cholesterol etc., **fats and oils**, you will be surprised to know, are actually a good source of energy and aid absorption of fat-soluble vitamins like A, E, D and K as well as provide lubrication to joints. Hence removing it drastically from our diet not only makes us fall prey to various vitamin and mineral deficiencies but also invites digestive problems, joint pains etc. This is the reason why nutritionists and health experts advise people to consume 3-4 teaspoons of oil per day.

The whole idea behind coming up with this new title **"Zero Oil Rotis and Subzis"** is not to totally preclude the intake of oil and ghee from your diet but just to restrict it to the prescribed limit per day and help balance your daily calorie intake. By including a zero oil roti and subzi as one meal in your daily diet, you can curb the intake of excess fats and calories. This helps you to enjoy both your favourite dishes and good health without worrying about an increasing waistline.

However, making zero oil recipes is not just about eliminating oil from your regular recipes and cooking them. It involves thorough research and effort to choose the right ingredients in the correct proportions and to develop an appropriate method of cooking. I have standardized and compiled **40** nutritious and delicious recipes of *rotis* and *subzis* along with my team of chefs and nutritionists after immense research and trials. This book offers you a selection of recipes from different cuisines, such as **Bharvan Baingan**, page 64, from Maharashtra, **Khatti Meethi Papdi**, page 67 from Gujarat and **Chole**, page 72, from Punjab, to provide you a wide variety of flavours.

Zero oil cooking is a skill, which I mastered as I wrote this book and you too can master it through practice and patience. With a well-chosen collection of delicious recipes, I am sure this book will change the pre-conceived notion about having to essentially add oodles of oil to make Indian cooking tasty, and to help you make your family's meal times healthier and happier.

Warm regards,

Tarla Dalal

CONTENTS

ROTIS AND PARATHAS

BASIC RECIPES

Cooking without oil can be a little difficult but definitely not impossible... With slight modifications in the method of cooking, its technique and ingredients, cooking becomes an easier, fun-filled, rather healthful experience. Given below are the modifications we have used and charted out for you all to learn and make your cooking easy...

A FEW COOKING TRICKS

1. **Using low fat ingredients -** The very foundation of diet control is in identifying and consuming the right ingredients. To curb the calories and fat we have used low fat milk and milk products like curds, *paneer*, and mozzarella cheese. They are low in calories compared to full-fat milk and milk-products yet they taste just as good. Low fat milk is easily available in the market as 99.9% fat-free under different brand names. Use this milk preferably as it is low in calories and fat, if you don't find you can use double-toned milk (slightly high in fat compared to 99.9% fat free milk). Remember that the regular toned available in the market is only 33.3% fat-free.

   Alternately you can make low fat milk at home, preparing low fat milk at home does not demand much effort. All you need to do is boil the milk and skim the fat (*malai*) that is formed after the milk cools. Repeat this procedure at least twice or thrice a day to get almost fat free milk.

   To keep a check on the calories without compromising on the original flavours of some traditional delicacies we have used moderate amounts of high-calorie foods like cashewnuts, coconut, poppy seeds etc., such as in recipes like ***Soya Tikkis in Malwani***

Gravy, page 18, Mushroom and Green Peas Curry, page 36, Vaal Dalimbi, page 47, Bhindi Masala, page 56, etc.

2. **Choosing and using healthy ingredients -** To make these recipes nutritious, I have used lots of healthy ingredients like fresh vegetables, whole wheat flour, soya flour, *nachni* flour etc. besides avoiding the use of oil. In addition to this, health and flavour are further enhanced by using ingredients like garlic paste, low fat curds, low fat *paneer*, coriander, lemon juice, steamed vegetables etc.

3. **Using vegetable stock -** Use of vegetable stock not only enhances the taste of any recipe but also increases its nutritional value manifold. We have used vegetable stock in place of water while making subzis. Refer to page 102, for the recipe of vegetable stock.

4. **Using non-stick cookware -** Use a non-stick pan/ *tava/ kadai* instead of the usual steel utensils. This ensures that the food does not stick to the utensil and burn, as there is no oil used. Non-stick cookware also prevents the *masala* from burning and cooking them on a slow flame enhances its taste and flavour. On the whole, using non-stick cookware, not only makes food healthier and tastier, but also makes cooking much easier! No more scraping the sides of vessels! Besides this, the wide range of cookware, pressure cookers, steamers etc. eases your cooking.

5. **Sprinkling water -** Sprinkling some water while cooking prevents the *masalas* and the vegetables from burning. What's more, it also helps to reduce the time required for cooking. It is amazing how such simple alterations provide multiple advantages!

6. **Roasting onions –** There is no contesting the lure of onion's flavour and strong smell. Roasting enhances these. Simply pierce an unpeeled onion with a fork and then roast it on an open flame for 5 to 10 minutes, turning it at regular intervals. Ensure that the flame is low and continue roasting till the outer layer is charred and black. Then, cool and discard the outermost layer and use as required.

7. **Roasting garlic –** Roasted garlic certainly adds value to any recipe, by enhancing the flavour and making it more appetising. Just pierce the unpeeled garlic cloves with a fork and roast them on an open flame for 4 to 5 minutes while turning at regular intervals. Here to, you should make sure that the flame is low. Continue roasting till the outer layer is charred and black. Cool and discard the outermost layer, use as required in the recipe, and be prepared to be dazzled by the enhanced flavour!

8. **Steaming –** Have you ever tried steaming *koftas* instead of frying or shallow-frying them? I did and they turned out to be extremely tasty! Now, you certainly don't have to abstain from *kofta curries* anymore. With regard to steaming, it's also worth remembering that discarding the water after boiling vegetables results in the loss of nutrients and flavour. To avoid this, we have steamed the vegetables, pressure-cooked or cooked them in just enough water. This technique is used in dishes like ***Subzi Pasanda**, page 24, **Vegetable Stew**, page 32, **Vaal Dalimbi**, page 47 etc.*

9. **Making wise use of spices –** To avoid the recipes from tasting over-spicy (which is likely to happen as spices are more potent when dry-roasted or when there is no oil used) I have reduced the amount of spices and condiments compared to what is normally used.

Tameta Muthia Nu Shaak

Traditionally Gujaratis make this recipe with oodles of oil, but you'll be surprised to know that I have made this subzi without any oil, yet maintaining the original flavour. So, soak in the richness of vitamin A and C in tomatoes without worrying about oil! To make this subzi in a jiffy make the muthias in advance and refrigerate them.

Preparation time: 20 minutes. Cooking time: 30 minutes. Serves 4.

For the *methi-doodhi muthia*

1 cup finely chopped fenugreek (*methi*) leaves
½ cup grated bottle gourd (*doodhi / lauki*)
¼ cup whole wheat flour (*gehun ka atta)*
2 tbsp *besan* (Bengal gram flour)
3 tbsp low fat curds (*dahi*), page 100
½ tsp ginger-green chilli paste
1 tsp sugar
1 tsp lemon juice

¼ tsp turmeric powder (*haldi*)
A pinch carom seeds (*ajwain*)
Salt to taste

Other ingredients
½ tsp mustard seeds (*rai / sarson*)
1 tsp grated ginger
4 to 5 curry leaves (*kadi patta*)
¼ tsp asafoetida (*hing*)
2 cups finely chopped tomatoes
1 tsp turmeric powder (*haldi*)
1 tbsp coriander-cumin seeds (*dhania-jeera*) powder
Salt to taste
2 tsp sugar (optional)
2 tbsp chopped coriander (*dhania*)

For the *methi-doodhi muthia*

1. Combine all the ingredients together in a bowl and knead into a soft dough adding 1 to 2 tbsp of water if required.
2. Divide it into 2 equal portions and shape each portion into a cylindrical roll of approx. 150 mm. (6") length and 25 mm. (1") diameter.

3. Steam in a steamer till done.
4. Cut into 12 mm. (½") slices and keep aside.

How to proceed

1. Heat a non-stick *kadhai* on a medium flame and when it is hot, add the mustard seeds and roast for 10 to 15 seconds.
2. Add the ginger, curry leaves and asafoetida and stir gently for about 10 seconds. Sprinkle little water if it starts burning.
3. Add the tomatoes, turmeric powder, coriander-cumin seeds powder and salt. Mix well, reduce the flame and simmer in a covered vessel for 10 to 12 minutes.
4. Add the sugar *methi-doodhi muthias* and 1 cup of water. Mix gently and bring to boil.
5. Simmer for 3 to 4 minutes and then add the coriander, mix again and heat for a minute.
   Serve hot.

Nutritive values per serving

Energy	Protein	Carbohydrates	Invisible Fat	Fibre	Vitamin A	Vitamin C
79 cal	3.1 gm	15.1 gm	0.6 gm	1.0 gm	576.6 mcg	27.3 mg

Lauki Kofta Curry

Gone are those days when you had to spend half a day in the kitchen preparing kofta curry! With this simple recipe, cooking becomes not only less tedious but also healthier as the koftas are steamed rather than fried. Cook the gravy on a medium flame to avoid burning of spices and onions. Highly recommended for heart patients as it is low in sodium and fat apart from being high in potassium.

Preparation time: 20 minutes. Cooking time: 40 minutes. Serves 4.

For the *lauki koftas*
½ cup grated bottle gourd *(doodhi / lauki)*
2 tbsp *besan* (Bengal gram flour)
1 small potato, boiled and mashed
½ tsp ginger-garlic paste
½ tsp green chilli paste
½ tsp *chaat masala*
Salt to taste

Other ingredients
2 roasted onions, page 11, roughly chopped

½ tsp chopped ginger
2 roasted garlic cloves, page 11, roughly chopped
2 tomatoes, blanched and roughly chopped
¼ tsp cumin seeds *(jeera)*
¼ tsp turmeric powder *(haldi)*
1 tsp chilli powder
½ tsp *garam masala*
1½ cups vegetable stock, page 102
Salt to taste
2 tbsp chopped coriander *(dhania)* for the garnish

For the *lauki koftas*

1. Combine all the ingredients together in a bowl.
2. Divide the mixture into 16 equal portions and shape them into small round *koftas*.
3. Steam in a steamer for about 20 minutes till the *koftas* are done. Keep aside.

How to proceed

1. Blend the onions, ginger and garlic to a smooth paste in a mixer. Keep aside.
2. Blend the tomatoes to a purée in a mixer.

3. Heat a non-stick *kadhai* on a medium flame and when it is hot, add the cumin seeds.
4. Dry roast for 10 to 15 seconds and then add the ground paste and cook stirring continuously till it turns brown in colour.
5. Add the tomato purée, turmeric powder, chilli powder, *garam masala,* vegetable stock and salt and simmer on a low flame for 10 minutes.
6. Add the *koftas* and simmer for 3 to 4 minutes.
   Serve hot garnished with coriander.

Handy tip : Ensure that you steam the *lauki koftas* as soon as they are made, otherwise the bottle gourd will leave water and make the *koftas* sticky.

Nutritive values per serving

Energy	Protein	Carbohydrates	Invisible Fat	Fibre	Sodium	Potassium
57 cal	1.9 gm	11.5 gm	0.4 gm	0.7 gm	12.1 mg	182.4 mg

Soya Tikkis in Malwani Gravy

Picture on facing page.

Malwani gravy in its original cooking style requires lots of coconut and oil, making it obviously high on the calorie scale! For a healthier version of this tasty subzi, use just 2 tbsp of coconut and lots of coriander. To make it even healthier, I have used tikkis made from soya granules and potatoes. Add the soya tikkis just before serving this delectable subzi as otherwise they will soak up all the gravy and become soggy.

Preparation time: 20 minutes. Cooking time: 30 minutes. Serves 4.

For the soya *tikkis*
1 cup soya nuggets
¼ cup grated carrots
1 potato, boiled and mashed
1 tsp finely chopped green chillies
Salt to taste

Other ingredients
2 tbsp grated fresh coconut
3 cloves roasted garlic, page 11
¼ cup chopped coriander (*dhania*)
1 whole dry kashmiri red chilli, dry roasted
25 mm. (1") piece ginger
¼ tsp turmeric powder (*haldi*)
2 roasted onions, page 11, finely chopped
Salt to taste

SOYA TIKKIS IN MALWANI GRAVY : Recipe above. →

For the soya *tikkis*

1. Grind the soya nuggets in a mixer to a coarse powder and soak them in hot water for 2 to 3 minutes. Strain and discard the water.
2. Squeeze and discard all the remaining water.
3. Add the carrots, potatoes, green chillies and salt and mix well.
4. Divide the mixture into 8 equal portions and shape each portion into a flat *tikki*.
5. Cook them on a hot non-stick pan till brown on both the sides. Keep aside.

How to proceed

1. Heat a thick iron *tava* (griddle) and when it is hot, add the coconut.
2. Dry roast for about 2 minutes or till brown while stirring continuously.
3. Add the garlic, coriander, red chilli, ginger, turmeric powder and half the onions and blend to a smooth paste in a mixer. Keep aside.
4. Heat a non-stick *kadhai* on a medium flame and when it is hot, add the remaining onions, prepared paste, salt and 1 cup of water and simmer for 8 to 10 minutes. Keep aside.
5. To serve, place the soya *tikkis* on a serving dish and pour the hot gravy on top. Serve hot.

Nutritive values per serving

Energy	Protein	Carbohydrates	Invisible Fat	Fibre	Vitamin A	Iron
117 cal	6.6 gm	11.7 gm	4.9 gm	1.0 gm	369.9 mcg	1.8 mg

Khatta Gobhi

My favourite vegetable, gobhi (cauliflower) is cooked in a different style in this sour curds gravy. Besides being low in calories this subzi is also nutritious as as it is brimming with the goodness of calcium. Relish this subzi with steaming hot parathas or rice, for a wholesome and delicious treat.

Preparation time: 15 minutes. Cooking time: 20 minutes. Serves 4.

For the paste

¼ cup freshly grated coconut
2 green chillies, roughly chopped
25 mm (1″) piece ginger, roughly chopped
4 tsp roasted *chana dal (daria)*
1 tsp cumin seeds *(jeera)*, dry roasted
Salt to taste

Other ingredients

¼ cup low fat curds *(dahi)*, page 100
½ cup low fat milk
¼ tsp turmeric powder *(haldi)*

1 cup vegetable stock, page 102
1 tsp mustard seeds *(rai / sarson)*
1 tsp *urad dal* (split black lentil)
5 curry leaves *(kadi patta)*
1 whole dry red chilli, broken into pieces
½ tsp *garam masala*
A pinch asafoetida *(hing)*
1½ cups cauliflower florets, boiled
Salt to taste
2 tbsp chopped coriander for the garnish

For the paste

Combine all the ingredients with 2 tbsp of water and blend to a smooth paste in a mixer. Keep aside.

How to proceed

1. Beat the curds and milk in a bowl till smooth, add the turmeric powder, vegetable stock and salt. Mix well and keep aside.
2. Combine the beaten curds with the prepared paste, mix well and keep aside.
3. Heat a non-stick *kadhai* on a medium flame and when it is hot, add the mustard

seeds, *urad dal,* curry leaves, red chillies, *garam masala* and asafoetida and dry roast them for 15 to 20 seconds.

4. Add the prepared curds mixture, mix well and bring to boil.
5. Add the cauliflower and salt and simmer for 8 to 10 minutes.

   Serve hot garnished with coriander.

Nutritive values per serving

Energy	Protein	Carbohydrates	Invisible Fat	Fibre	Calcium
43 cal	2.1 gm	4.1 gm	2.0 gm	0.4 gm	47.7 mg

Subzi Pasanda

True to the name, "Subzi Pasanda" is a veggie dish you will love! Calorie-laden cashewnut paste is replaced with a healthy paste made with cauliflower and onions. Both, the use of mixed vegetables and the vegetable stock, perks up the flavour.

Preparation time: 15 minutes. Cooking time: 20 minutes. Serves 4.

For the paste
2 cups sliced onions
½ small cauliflower, finely chopped
1 to 2 green chillies, chopped
2 large cloves garlic, chopped
12 mm. (½") piece ginger, sliced
1 stick cinnamon (*dalchini*)
1 clove (*laung / lavang*)
1 cup low fat milk

Other ingredients
½ cup low fat milk
¼ cup fresh low fat curds (*dahi*), page 100

1 tbsp *besan* (Bengal gram flour)
¼ tsp cumin seeds (*jeera*)
½ tsp dried fenugreek leaves (*kasuri methi*)
¼ tsp *garam masala*
Salt to taste
1½ cups vegetable stock, page 102
2 cups steamed mixed vegetables (carrots, French beans, potatoes, cauliflower, green peas)
2 tbsp chopped coriander (*dhania*) for the garnish

For the paste

1. Combine all the ingredients in a non-stick *kadhai* and simmer for 8 to 10 minutes till the onions are soft and nearly all the liquid has evaporated.
2. Remove and discard the cinnamon and clove.
3. Blend the mixture to a smooth paste in a mixer. Keep aside.

How to proceed

1. Whisk the milk, curds and *besan* in a small bowl and keep aside.
2. Heat a non-stick *kadhai* on a medium flame and when it is hot, add the cumin seeds.

3. Dry roast for 10 to 15 seconds and then add the dried fenugreek leaves and cook, stirring continuously, for 10 more seconds.
4. Add the prepared paste, milk-curd-*besan* mixture, *garam masala*, salt and ½ cup of vegetable stock and bring the mixture to boil.
5. Add the vegetables and the remaining vegetable stock and simmer for another 3 to 4 minutes.

Serve hot garnished with coriander.

Handy tip: Remember to use fresh curds as sour curds will require the addition of sugar, thereby increasing calories.

Nutritive values per serving

Energy	Protein	Carbohydrates	Invisible Fat	Fibre	Calcium
96 cal	5.5 gm	17.5 gm	0.4 gm	1.2 gm	187.2 mg

Cauliflower Indad

Picture on back cover.

Yet another dish made with the versatile cauliflower. Since gobhi has a bland flavour, it can go well with any gravy and combination of spices. Here is a wonderful treat for all you spice lovers. To enhance the dish's allure, use fresh cauliflower and keep the florets slightly big in size.

Preparation time: 15 minutes. Cooking time: 20 minutes. Serves 4.

½ tsp cumin seeds *(jeera)*
4 peppercorns
25 mm. (1") piece cinnamon (*dalchini*)
2 whole cardamoms (*elaichi*)
2 cloves (*laung / lavang*)
4 whole dry red chillies, broken into pieces
1 roasted onion, page 11, finely chopped
3 cloves garlic
½ tsp turmeric powder *(haldi)*
1 tsp ginger-green chilli paste
Salt to taste
2 cup blanched cauliflower florets

½ tsp tamarind *(imli)* paste
1 tsp vinegar
2 tbsp finely chopped coriander *(dhania)* for the garnish

1. Heat a thick iron *tava* (griddle) on a medium flame and when hot, add the cumin seeds, peppercorn, cinnamon, cardamoms, cloves and roast for about 10 seconds.
2. Add the red chillies and roast for 10 more seconds.
3. Add the onions, garlic, turmeric powder, ginger-green chilli paste and ¼ cup of water and blend to a smooth paste in a mixer.
4. Heat a non-stick *kadhai* on a medium flame and when hot, add the paste and salt and dry roast for 3 to 4 minutes while stirring continuously
5. Add the cauliflower, tamarind paste, vinegar, 1 cup of water and bring to boil.
6. Simmer for about 5 minutes and serve hot garnished with coriander.

Nutritive values per serving

Energy	Protein	Carbohydrates	Invisible Fat	Fibre
21 cal	1.2 gm	3.6 gm	0.2 gm	0.6 gm

Kofta Makhani

The very word 'makhani' brings to our mind lots of butter and cream! But here I have created the same rich and creamy effect with low fat milk mixed with cornflour. Vibrant, red-coloured koftas made using beetroot and carrots not only add colour to this subzi but also add nutrients like vitamin A, fibre and folic acid.

Preparation time: 20 minutes. Cooking time: 30 minutes. Serves 4.

For the *koftas*
1 cup grated beetroot
1 cup grated carrot
½ cup *besan* (Bengal gram flour)
½ potato, boiled and mashed
1 tsp ginger-garlic paste
1 tsp chilli powder
1 tsp *chaat masala*
Salt to taste

For the *makhani* gravy
3 cups chopped tomatoes
½ cup chopped onions
2 large cloves garlic, chopped
12 mm. (½") piece ginger, chopped
2 cloves *(laung / lavang)*
1 stick cinnamon *(dalchini)*
¼ cup chopped red pumpkin *(kaddu)*
1 whole dry Kashmiri red chilli, broken into pieces

Other ingredients
½ tsp cumin seeds *(jeera)*
¼ tsp dried fenugreek leaves (*kasuri methi*)
½ tsp chilli powder

½ tsp sugar
Salt to taste
½ tsp cornflour dissolved in ½ cup low fat milk
2 tbsp chopped coriander *(dhania)* for the garnish

For the *koftas*

1. Combine all the ingredients together in a bowl.
2. Divide the mixture into 12 equal portions and shape each portion into a small round *kofta*.
3. Steam in a steamer for about 20 minutes till the *koftas* are firm. Keep aside.

For the *makhani* gravy

1. Combine all the ingredients along with ¾ cup of water in a *kadhai* and heat over a medium flame till the vegetables are tender.
2. Allow to cool completely and discard the cloves and cinnamon.
3. Blend the mixture to a smooth purée in a mixer. Keep aside.

How to proceed

1. Heat a non-stick *kadhai* on a medium flame and when hot add the cumin seeds and dry roast for about 10 seconds.
2. Add the dried fenugreek leaves and chilli powder and cook while stirring continuously for 5 to 10 seconds. If the chilli powder starts burning, sprinkle a little water over it.
3. Add the *makhani* gravy, sugar and salt and bring it to boil.
4. Add the cornflour-milk mixture and simmer for 4 to 5 minutes.
5. Add the *koftas* and simmer for 2 to 3 minutes.

   Serve hot garnished with coriander.

Nutritive values per serving

Energy	Protein	Carbohydrates	Invisible Fat	Fibre	Vitamin A	Folic Acid
104 cal	4.8 gm	19.0 gm	0.9 gm	1.5 gm	1012.3 mcg	57.0 mcg

Vegetable Stew

Easy-to-make, yet deliciousnow that's a good combination of attributes for a recipe! Cooking dinner can be tiresome after a hectic day, but here is a healthy and yummy dinner which you can whip up in a matter of minutes with the vegetables and whole wheat bread stocked in your refrigerator. Use any vegetables of your choice.

Preparation time: 15 minutes. Cooking time: 20 minutes. Serves 4.

2 tbsp plain flour (*maida*)
2 cups vegetable stock, page 102
2 onions, cut into cubes
2 peppercorns
1 clove (*laung / lavang*)
1 stick cinnamon (*dalchini*)
1½ tsp chopped garlic
2 tbsp chopped celery
1 cup carrot cubes
½ cup *tendli*, quartered
Salt to taste
1 cup sliced mushrooms (*khumbh*)

1. Dissolve the plain flour in ¼ cup of vegetable stock. Keep aside.
2. Heat a non-stick sauce pan on a medium flame and when hot, add the onions.
3. Dry roast for sometime while stirring continuously till they are lightly browned.
4. Add the peppercorns, clove and cinnamon and dry roast for another minute while continuing to stir.
5. Add the garlic, celery, carrots, *tendli,* salt and the remaining vegetable stock and cook on a low flame till the vegetables are tender.
6. Add the mushrooms and simmer for 3 to 4 minutes.
7. Add the plain flour-vegetable stock mixture and bring to boil, while stirring continuously so that no lumps remain.
8. Allow to simmer for 5 to 7 minutes adding a little water if required.

Serve hot.

Nutritive values per serving

Energy	Protein	Carbohydrates	Invisible Fat	Fibre	Vitamin A
49 cal	1.9 gm	10.4 gm	0.2 gm	0.8 gm	298.9 mcg

Baby Corn Palak

Spinach and baby corn blend with in this scrumptious and nutritious dish. Spinach provides lots of calcium while baby corn provides fibre. To retain the bright green colour of spinach, ensure that you blanch it just for a few minutes and do not over cook it.

Preparation time: 15 minutes.   Cooking time: 10 minutes.   Serves 4.

2 roasted onions, page 11, roughly chopped
1 tsp grated ginger
1 green chilli, roughly chopped
¾ cup blanched spinach *(palak)*, refer to handy tip
2 tbsp fresh low fat curds *(dahi)*, page 100
2 tbsp low fat milk
7 to 8 baby corn, blanched and cut into 25 mm. (1″) pieces
A pinch turmeric powder *(haldi)*
1 tsp dry mango powder *(amchur)*
¼ tsp *garam masala*
½ tsp dried fenugreek leaves *(kasuri methi)*, roasted
Salt to taste

1. Heat a non-stick *kadhai* on a medium flame and when hot, add the onions, ginger and green chillies.
2. Dry roast for 2 to 3 minutes while stirring continuously.
3. Add the spinach, curds, milk and ½ cup of water and blend in a mixer to a smooth paste.
4. Pour the mixture back into the *kadhai*, add the baby corn, turmeric powder, dry mango powder, *garam masala*, dried fenugreek leaves, salt and ½ cup of water and bring to boil.
5. Simmer for 4 to 5 minutes and serve hot.

Handy tip : To get ¾ cup of blanched spinach, add 3½ cups of chopped spinach to a vesselful of hot water and cook for 3 to 4 minutes. Then drain, squeeze out all the water and wash in ice -cold water.

Nutritive values per serving

Energy	Protein	Carbohydrates	Invisible Fat	Fibre	Calcium	Vitamin C
77 cal	3.6 gm	16.0 gm	0.5 gm	1.6 gm	85.7 mg	22.7 mg

Mushroom and Green Peas Curry

Picture on facing page.

Very popular with my grandchildren, this curry is best relished with steaming hot phulkas. Both mushrooms and green peas are a storehouse of nutrients like fibre, zinc, potassium, folic acid etc. Making zero oil subzi is not as difficult as it may sound, as it does not totally prevent you from adding sinful ingredients like cashewnuts, coconut, etc. but just requires you to use them moderately.

Preparation time: 15 minutes. Cooking time: 15 minutes. Serves 4.

To be ground into a paste

2 tbsp chopped cashewnuts
2 tbsp poppy seeds (*khus-khus*), soaked in 2 tbsp of water
2 green chillies, roughly chopped
2 cloves (*laung / lavang*)
2 cloves garlic
2 cardamoms (*elaichi*)
1 tsp chopped ginger

MUSHROOM AND GREEN PEAS CURRY : Recipe above →
and CAULIFLOWER ROTI, Recipe on page 86.

Other ingredients

½ cup chopped onions
2 cups vegetable stock, page 102
1 cup green peas
Salt to taste
1½ cups sliced mushrooms (*khumbh*)
¼ cup fresh low fat curds (*dahi*), page 100
¼ cup low fat milk
2 tbsp chopped coriander (*dhania*) for the garnish

1. Heat a non-stick pan on a medium flame and when hot, add the ground paste.
2. Cook while stirring continuously till it is light brown in colour. Sprinkle a little water if the paste burns.
3. Add the onions and dry roast while stirring continuously till they turn translucent.
4. Add ½ cup of vegetable stock to it and mix well till smooth. Keep aside.
5. Heat a non-stick *kadhai* on a medium flame and when hot, add the peas, salt and the remaining vegetable stock.
6. When it starts boiling, add the ground paste and simmer till the peas get cooked.
7. Add the mushrooms, curds and milk and simmer for another 5 minutes.

Serve hot garnished with coriander.

Nutritive values per serving

Energy	Protein	Carbohydrates	Invisible Fat	Fibre	Zinc	Potassium
128 cal	7.2 gm	14.1 gm	4.9 gm	2.0 gm	1.0 mg	143.2 mg

Shahi Paneer Mutter

The word 'shahi' is immediately associated with rich, fat-laden and royal subzis. Here is a healthier version of the same, made with well-chosen ingredients and slight modifications to the cooking style. You will be surprised to note it retains the royal flavour! To maintain the richness and the taste of this shahi subzi I have used low fat milk and 1 tbsp of cashewnut purée.

Preparation time: 10 minutes. Cooking time: 20 minutes. Serves 4.

¾ cup onion purée
2 tbsp cashewnut purée
1 tsp garlic paste
½ cup low fat milk
½ tsp dried fenugreek leaves (*kasuri methi*), roasted
½ tsp *garam masala*
Salt to taste
¾ cup low fat *paneer* (cottage cheese) cubes, page 101
¼ cup boiled peas
2 tbsp chopped coriander *(dhania)* for the garnish

1. Heat a non-stick *kadhai* on a medium flame and when hot, add the onion purée and dry roast while stirring continuously.
2. Add the cashewnut purée and garlic paste and dry roast for 5 to 7 minutes or till brown in colour while stirring continuously.
3. Add ½ cup water and mix well to get a smooth mixture like paste.
4. Add the milk, dried fenugreek leaves, *garam masala* and salt, mix well and bring to boil.
5. Simmer for 2 to 3 minutes.
6. Add the *paneer* and peas and mix gently.
   Serve hot garnished with coriander.

Handy tip : To make ¾ cup onion purée, just chop 2 onions roughly and blend them in a mixer till smooth.

Nutritive values per serving

Energy	Protein	Carbohydrates	Invisible Fat	Fibre	Vitamin A	Calcium
180 cal	11.7 gm	25.7 gm	2.2 gm	0.7 gm	1019.5 mcg	571.0 mg

Nawabi Aloo

Picture on page 1

Despite the 'couch potato' allusion, potatoes are actually quite healthy if not deep-fried. If boiled or cooked without oil like in this recipe, the goodness of potatoes is really tapped. A real delicacy, this recipe lets you take advantage of the rich potassium content in potato, without worrying about an increasing waistline as the side effect!

Preparation time: 15 minutes. Cooking time: 30 minutes. Serves 4.

2 boiled potatoes, peeled and cubed
1½ cups chopped tomatoes
½ tsp sugar
½ cup low fat milk
Salt to taste

To be ground into a smooth paste
2 roasted onions, page 11, roughly chopped
½ tbsp coriander (*dhania*) seeds
½ tbsp cumin seeds *(jeera)*
½ tbsp poppy seeds (*khus-khus*), soaked in tbsp of water
1 tsp fennel seeds (*saunf*)

25 mm. (1") piece ginger, roughly chopped
2 green chillies, roughly chopped
1 tsp cardamom (*elaichi*) powder

1. Heat a non-stick pan on a medium flame and when hot, add the potatoes.
2. Dry roast till the potatoes are brown from all the sides. Keep aside.
3. Put the tomatoes and 1 cup of water in a non-stick *kadhai* and cook for about 10 minutes. Cool completely.
4. Blend in a mixer to a smooth purée. Keep aside.
5. Heat the non-stick *kadhai* again on a medium flame and when hot, add the ground paste and cook for 2 to 3 minutes while stirring continuously.
6. Add the tomato purée, potatoes, sugar, milk and salt and simmer for 5 to 7 minutes.

   Serve hot.

Nutritive values per serving

Energy	Protein	Carbohydrates	Invisible Fat	Fibre	Calcium	Potassium
81 cal	2.7 gm	16.4 gm	0.5 gm	0.8 gm	110.1 mg	217.6 mg

Masoor Masala

Masoor, a very nutritious lentil, is also very pleasing to the palate. Cooked in well-chosen spices, this subzi is not only tasty but also brims with protein, iron and folic acid. It goes well with cooked rice. Soaking masoor dal overnight not only reduces the cooking time but also makes it easily digestible.

Preparation time: 15 minutes. Cooking time: 20 minutes. Serves 4.
Soaking time: Overnight.

1 cup *masoor dal* (split red lentil), soaked overnight
½ tsp cumin seeds (*jeera*)
1 bayleaf (*tejpatta*)
1 roasted onion, page 11, finely chopped
¾ cup finely chopped tomatoes
1 tsp ginger-garlic paste
¼ tsp turmeric powder (*haldi*)
½ tsp chilli powder
½ tsp *garam masala*
Salt to taste

2 tbsp chopped coriander *(dhania)* for the garnish

1. Wash and drain the *masoor dal*. Keep aside
2. Add 1 cup of water and salt to the *dal* and pressure cook it for 1 whistle. Keep aside.
3. Heat a non-stick *kadhai* on a medium flame and when hot, add the cumin seeds, bayleaf and onions and roast on a slow flame while stirring continuously till it turns golden brown in colour.
4. Add the tomatoes and cook while continuing to stir for 5 to 7 minutes or till done.
5. Add ginger-garlic paste, turmeric powder, chilli powder, *garam masala*, salt and *masoor dal* with the water and mix well.
6. Simmer on a slow flame for 5 to 6 minutes.
   Serve hot garnished with coriander.

Nutritive values per serving

Energy	Protein	Carbohydrates	Invisible Fat	Fibre	Iron	Folic Acid
151 cal	10.2 gm	26.6 gm	0.4 gm	1.3 gm	3.3 mg	24.1 mcg

Aloo Mutter Korma

The traditional aloo-mutter combination is here in a new zero oil avatar, tasty as ever! Refrigerate boiled potatoes and boiled green peas and make this subzi in just a few minutes anytime you wish to. Since green peas are crammed with fibre, it is indeed a health treat for your heart, as fibre helps to remove excess fat (cholesterol) from the body.

Preparation time: 15 minutes. Cooking time: 20 minutes. Serves 4.

½ tsp cumin seeds (*jeera*)
½ cup chopped onions
½ tsp ginger-green chilli paste
½ tsp garlic paste
1 cup chopped tomatoes
A pinch turmeric powder (*haldi*)
½ tsp chilli powder
½ tsp *garam masala*
½ tsp sugar
1 cup boiled fresh green peas
1½ cups potatoes, boiled, peeled and cut into cubes
1 cup vegetable stock, page 102

Salt to taste
1 tbsp chopped coriander *(dhania)* for the garnish

1. Heat a non-stick *kadhai* on a medium flame and when hot, add the cumin seeds and dry roast for about 10 seconds.
2. Add the onions and cook till they turn brown while stirring continuously.
3. Add the ginger-green chilli paste, garlic paste and tomatoes and simmer till the tomatoes are cooked.
4. Add the turmeric powder, chilli powder, *garam masala*, sugar, peas and potatoes and cook for 4 to 5 minutes.
5. Add the vegetable stock and salt and simmer till the gravy thickens.
   Serve hot garnished with coriander.

Nutritive values per serving

Energy	Protein	Carbohydrates	Invisible Fat	Fibre	Potassium
89 cal	3.9 gm	17.9 gm	0.2 gm	2.1 gm	194.3 mg

Vaal Dalimbi

Most Maharashtrian subzis are made using lots of coconut paste. Here's a delicious but healthy exception that uses only 2 tbsp of coconut, thereby making it low in calories and fat. Sprouting vaal helps increase its vitamin and mineral content and makes it easily digestible too.

Preparation time: 15 minutes. Cooking time: 20 minutes. Serves 4.
Soaking time: Overnight.

For the paste
1 roasted onion, page 11, sliced
2 tbsp freshly grated coconut
½ tsp coriander *(dhania)* seeds
½ tsp cumin seeds *(jeera)*
¼ tsp jaggery *(gur)*
3 tsp tamarind *(imli)* water

Other ingredients
1 cup sprouted *vaal* (field beans)
25 mm (1") piece cinnamon *(dalchini)*
1 bayleaf *(tejpatta)*
1 clove *(laung / lavang)*
A pinch of asafoetida *(hing)*
¼ tsp mustard seeds *(rai / surson)*
¼ tsp turmeric powder *(haldi)*
1 tbsp chilli powder
½ tsp *garam masala*
Salt to taste
¼ tsp sugar
2 tbsp chopped coriander *(dhania)* for the garnish

For the paste

1. Heat a non-stick pan on a medium flame and when hot, add the all the ingredients and dry roast while stirring continuously till the coconut turns brown.
2. Cool, add 2 tbsp of water and blend in a mixer to a smooth paste.

How to proceed

1. Wash and drain the *vaal* and pressure cook for 1 whistle. Allow the sream to escape and then drain and keep aside.
2. Heat a non-stick *kadhai* on a medium flame and when hot, add the cinnamon, bayleaf, clove, asafoetida and mustard seeds and dry roast for about 30 seconds.
3. Add the *vaal*, turmeric powder, chilli powder, *garam masala* and salt and continue dry roasting for 5 minutes while stirring continuously. Sprinkle a little water if required.
4. Add the ground paste, sugar and 1 cup of water and simmer for 10 minutes. Serve hot garnished with coriander.

Nutritive values per serving

Energy	Protein	Carbohydrates	Invisible Fat	Fibre	Calcium
84 cal	3.9 gm	11.8 gm	2.4 gm	0.5 gm	21.0 mg

Rajma Saagwala

Rajma's versatility needs no introduction. It fits beautifully into quite a range of recipes! Here it combines with healthy amaranth leaves, which are rich in fibre, folic acid and vitamin C.

Preparation time: 15 minutes. Cooking time: 20 minutes. Serves 4.
Soaking time: Overnight.

½ cup *rajma* (kidney beans), soaked overnight
Salt to taste
½ tsp cumin seeds *(jeera)*
2 to 3 green chillies, chopped
½ tsp chopped ginger
½ tsp chopped garlic
½ cup chopped onions
3 cups chopped amaranth *(chawli)* leaves
¼ tsp turmeric powder *(haldi)*

¼ cup low fat milk
¼ tsp sugar (optional)

1. Wash and drain the *rajma*. Pressure cook them with 1 cup of water and salt for 2 to 3 whistles.
2. Allow the steam to escape before opening. Drain, discard the water and keep aside.
3. Heat a non-stick *kadhai* on a medium flame and when hot, add the cumin seeds.
4. Dry roast for about 30 seconds and then add the green chillies, ginger, garlic and onions and cook while stirring continuously till the onions turn brown.
5. Add the *rajma*, amaranth leaves and turmeric powder and mix well.
6. Add the milk and sugar and simmer for 5 to 7 more minutes.

   Serve hot.

Nutritive values per serving

Energy	Protein	Carbohydrates	Invisible Fat	Fibre	Folic Acid	Vitamin C
109 cal	7.6 gm	18.3 gm	0.6 gm	1.7 gm	102.3 mcg	39.1 mg

Tinda Masala

Healthy, easy-to-make and extremely tasty, this is the perfect way to cook the reasonably exotic tinda! Onions, tomatoes and spices, together they work their own magic in this dish, which tastes great with Besan Parathas, page 92.

Preparation time: 20 minutes.   Cooking time: 20 minutes.   Serves 4.

1 cup chopped onions
1 cup chopped tomatoes
1 tsp ginger-garlic paste
2 tsp coriander *(dhania)* powder
1 tsp cumin seeds *(jeera)* powder
½ tsp turmeric powder *(haldi)*
2 cups peeled and thinly sliced *tinda*
Salt to taste

1. Heat a non-stick *kadhai* on a medium flame and when hot, add the onions and dry roast them till they turn brown.
2. Add the tomatoes, ginger-garlic paste, coriander powder, cumin seeds powder,

turmeric powder, salt and 1 tbsp of water and cook for 3 to 4 minutes while stirring continuously.

3. Add the *tinda* and ½ cup water and cook covered on a low flame till the *tinda* is tender.
4. Remove the lid and increase the flame so all the water is evaporated.

Serve hot.

Nutritive values per serving

Energy	Protein	Carbohydrates	Invisible Fat	Fibre	Iron
35 cal	1.4 gm	6.8 gm	0.2 gm	1.0 gm	0.9 mg

Mava Mutter

Picture on page 55.

Mava (khoya) is extremely high in calories and fat, enough to scare the weight-watchers! Here I use low-calorie mava, which I made by adding some lime juice to low fat milk to get the actual grainy texture. Milk enhances the nutritive value of this subzi by providing protein and calcium. Try your own variations of this recipe by using other vegetables in place of green peas.

Preparation time: 10 minutes. Cooking time: 25 minutes. Serves 4.

For the *mava* (khoya)
½ tsp cornflour
2 cups low fat milk
½ tsp lemon juice

Other ingredients
2 pinch of asafoetida *(hing)*
2 green chillies, slit
1 tsp coriander *(dhania)* powder
1 tsp ginger-garlic paste
½ tsp *garam masala*
2 cup boiled fresh green peas
Salt to taste
2 tbsp chopped coriander *(dhania)* for the garnish

For the *mava* (khoya)

1. Dissolve the cornflour in ¼ cup of milk and keep aside.
2. Boil the remaining milk in a non-stick pan.
3. Reduce the flame, add the lemon juice and heat till the milk starts curdling.
4. Add the cornflour and milk mixture and continue cooking on a low flame, while stirring continuously, till all the water dries up and the colour changes to light brown. Keep aside.

How to proceed

1. Heat a non-stick *kadhai* on a medium flame and when hot, add the asafoetida, green chillies, coriander powder, ginger-garlic paste and *garam masala.*
2. Dry roast for about a minute. Sprinkle a little water if the mixture starts burning.
3. Add the green peas, *mava,* salt and 2 tbsp of water and cook for few minutes. Serve hot garnished with coriander.

Nutritive values per serving

Energy	Protein	Carbohydrates	Invisible Fat	Fibre	Calcium
111 cal	9.3 gm	18.0 gm	0.2 gm	3.2 gm	169.2 mg

MAVA MUTTER : Recipe on page 53. →

Bhindi Masala

Bhindi masala always brings to mind a yummy dish, literally floating in oil! I am sure many of you must have refrained from indulging in this subzi because of its obviously high oil-content. Not any more. Here is a healthier, oil-free version of bhindi masala that tastes equally great. Use roasted masalas, and cook the bhindi in a pressure cooker before roasting them in a non-stick kadhai.

Preparation time: 20 minutes. Cooking time: 10 minutes. Serves 4.

20 to 22 *bhindi* (ladies finger)

To be ground into a smooth paste
1 roasted onion, page 11, roughly chopped
2 tbsp freshly grated coconut
1 cup chopped coriander *(dhania)*
4 tsp sugar
2 tsp ginger-green chilli paste
1 tsp tumeric powder *(haldi)*
1 tbsp coriander-cumin seeds (*dhania-jeera*) powder
2 tsp *garam masala*

2 tsp roasted sesame seeds *(til)*
2 tbsp lemon juice
Salt to taste

1. Wash and pat dry the *bhindis.* Slit them lengthwise.
2. Stuff the *bhindi* with the prepared paste. Keep aside.
3. Pressure cook the stuffed *bhindi* and the remaining paste, if any, for 1 whistle.
4. Allow the steam to escape and then open the pressure cooker.
5. Heat a non-stick *kadhai* on a medium flame and when hot, add the *bhindi* and cook on a low flame for 5 to 6 minutes or till they are done.

   Serve hot.

Nutritive values per serving

Energy	Protein	Carbohydrates	Invisible Fat	Fibre	Vitamin C
76 cal	1.5 gm	10.9 gm	2.9 gm	0.9 gm	17.0 mg

Tandoori Mushrooms

Now, here's a healthy dish you are going to fall head-over-heels in love with! Mushrooms are low in calories and a valuable source of protein and folic acid. Folic acid protects the heart from the harmful action of an amino acid called homocysteine, and is essential for the formation of new red blood cells. If you're not very fond of mushrooms, try using low-fat paneer or baby corn pieces instead.

Preparation time: 10 minutes. Cooking time: 10 minutes. Serves 4.

300 grams mushrooms *(khumbh)*, cut into halves
½ tsp cornflour
½ cup low fat milk
½ tsp dried fenugreek leaves (*kasuri methi*)
¼ cup low fat curds (*dahi*), page 100, beaten
Salt to taste

To be ground into a smooth paste
4 whole dry Kashmiri red chillies
4 large cloves garlic
25 mm. (1") piece ginger

2 tsp coriander-cumin seeds *(dhania-jeera)* powder
Salt to taste

1. Wash the mushrooms thoroughly. Drain and keep aside.
2. Dissolve the cornflour in the milk and keep aside.
3. Heat a non-stick pan on a medium flame and when hot, add the prepared paste and dried fenugreek leaves and cook while stirring continuously for 1 minute. Sprinkle little water if the mixture becomes too dry.
4. Add the mushrooms, cornflour-milk mixture, curds and salt and sauté for 4 to 5 minutes till the mixture coats the mushrooms.
   Serve hot.

Nutritive values per serving

Energy	Protein	Carbohydrates	Invisible Fat	Fibre	Calcium	Folic Acid
33 cal	2.9 gm	5.5 gm	0.4 gm	1.0 gm	60.1 mg	15.9 mcg

Chawli Bhaji

Chawli, a pulse rich in fibre, folic acid and iron is here to please your palate with its unique taste and flavour. Tamarind and jaggery imparts a tangy and sweet flavour and make this bhaji a must try.

Preparation time: 10 minutes. Cooking time: 20 minutes. Serves 4.
Soaking time: Overnight.

1½ cups *chawli* (black eyed beans), soaked
Salt to taste
½ tsp cumin seeds (*jeera*)
¼ tsp asafoetida (*hing*)
¼ tsp turmeric powder (*haldi*)
1 tsp chilli powder
1 tsp coriander-cumin seeds (*dhania-jeera*) powder
2 tsp thick tamarind (*imli*) pulp
1 tbsp grated jaggery (*gur*)
2 tbsp chopped coriander *(dhania)* for the garnish

1. Drain the *chawli*, wash and drain again.
2. Add 2 cups of water and salt and pressure cook for 2 whistles.
3. Allow the steam to escape before opening. Drain the *chawli* and keep the liquid aside.
4. Heat a non-stick *kadhai* on a medium flame and when hot, add the cumin seeds, asafoetida and dry roast for about 30 seconds.
5. Add the *chawli*, 1 cup of liquid, turmeric powder, chilli powder, coriander-cumin seeds powder and salt and simmer for about 10 minutes.
6. Add the tamarind pulp and jaggery and bring to boil.

   Serve hot garnished with coriander.

Nutritive values per serving

Energy	Protein	Carbohydrates	Invisible Fat	Fibre	Folic Acid	Iron
212 cal	14.5 gm	36.8 gm	0.6 gm	2.3 gm	79.8 mcg	5.3 mg

Makai Jalfrazie

Picture on cover.

Though slightly time-consuming, this subzi is definitely worth the effort. Capsicum is a good source of vitamin C, an antioxidant that fights disease-causing free radicals and boosts our immune system while corn increases the allure of this dish manifold!

Preparation time: 10 minutes. Cooking time: 15 minutes. Serves 4.

3 spring onion whites, sliced
½ green capsicum, sliced
½ yellow capsicum, sliced
½ red capsicum, sliced
¾ cup boiled sweet corn kernels *(makai ke dane)*
¾ cup boiled white corn kernels *(makai ke dane)*
4 to 5 blanched baby corn, cut into 25 mm. (1") pieces
¼ tsp turmeric powder (*haldi*)
½ tsp chilli powder
½ tsp coriander-cumin seeds (*dhania-jeera*) powder
1 tomato, sliced
2 tbsp tomato ketchup

2 tbsp tomato purée
Salt to taste
3 spring onion greens, chopped
2 tsp vinegar
½ tsp *garam masala*
2 pinches sugar
2 tbsp chopped coriander (*dhania*) for the garnish

1. Heat a non-stick pan on a medium flame and when hot, add the spring onion whites and capsicums and dry roast for 2 minutes while stirring continuously.
2. Lower the flame, add the sweet corn kernels, white corn kernels, baby corn, turmeric powder, chilli powder, coriander-cumin seeds powder, tomatoes, tomato ketchup, tomato purée and salt and continue cooking for 2 to 3 minutes while stirring continuously. Sprinkle a little water if required.
3. Add the spring onion greens, vinegar, *garam masala* and sugar and toss lightly. Serve hot garnished with coriander.

Nutritive values per serving

Energy	Protein	Carbohydrates	Invisible Fat	Fibre	Vitamin C
135 cal	5.5 gm	29.3 gm	0.7 gm	3.8 gm	43.3 mg

Bharvan Baingan

Picture on facing page.

Stuffing them with spices and besan really enhances the flavour of brinjals in this dish! This subzi is easy and quick to make, as long as you have a pressure cooker on hand. Use the small and dark varieties of brinjal as they have a mild sweetness which combines well with the stuffing.

Preparation time: 20 minutes. Cooking time: 20 minutes. Serves 4.

8 *baingan* (small brinjal dark variety)
2 tbsp chopped coriander *(dhania)* for the garnish

For the paste
2 tbsp coriander *(dhania)* seeds
2 tbsp cumin seeds *(jeera)*
2 tsp chilli powder
2 tsp dry mango powder (*amchur*)
2 tsp sugar
2 tbsp *besan* (Bengal gram flour)
½ cup chopped coriander *(dhania)*

BHARVAN BAINGAN : Recipe above. →

For the paste

Blend all the ingredients to a smooth paste using a little water if required. Keep aside.

How to proceed

1. Slit each brinjal into four equal parts lengthwise without separating the pieces from the steam. Keep aside.
2. Stuff them with the prepared paste and put them in a pressure cooker. If any paste is left, spread it over the stuffed brinjals.
3. Pressure cook for 2 whistles.
4. Allow the steam escape and then open the pressure cooker. Keep aside.
5. Heat a non-stick *kadhai* and cook the stuffed brinjals in it on a low flame for 5 to 6 minutes or till they are tender.

   Serve hot garnished with coriander.

Nutritive values per serving

Energy	Protein	Carbohydrates	Invisible Fat	Fibre	Vitamin A	Vitamin C
41 cal	1.8 gm	7.4 gm	0.4 gm	0.8 gm	579.8 mcg	16.7 mg

Khatti Meethi Papdi

This delicacy is very commonly made in Gujarati households. Marinating papdi helps enhance the flavour, as the spices mix well with the papdi. Besan dhoklis increase the taste and appeal of the subzi, but remember to drop the dhoklis after the papdis are cooked. It is also important to simmer the subzi till the dhoklis get cooked. Papdi is rich in iron and thus helps increase haemoglobin count if consumed regularly.

Preparation time: 15 minutes. Cooking time: 15 minutes. Serves 4.

For the *besan* dumplings

½ cup *besan* (Bengal gram flour)
2 tbsp low fat curds (*dahi*), page 100, mixed with 2 tbsp water
¼ tsp chilli powder
A pinch turmeric powder (*haldi*)
Salt to taste

Other ingredients

25 to 30 *papdis*
¼ tsp turmeric powder (*haldi*)
1 tsp chilli powder

2 tsp coriander-cumin seeds (*dhania-jeera*) powder
1½ tbsp grated jaggery (*gur*)
A pinch asafoetida (*hing*)
Salt to taste
A pinch carom seeds (*ajwain*)

For the *besan* dumplings

Combine all the ingredients together in a bowl and whisk to make a smooth batter. Keep aside.

How to proceed

1. Remove the strings from the *papdis* and cut them into 50 mm. (2") long pieces.
2. Combine the *papdi*, turmeric powder, chilli powder, coriander-cumin seeds powder, jaggery, asafoetida and salt together in a bowl and keep aside to marinate for half an hour.
3. Heat a non-stick *kadhai* on a medium flame and when hot, add the carom seeds and dry roast on a slow flame for about 10 seconds.
4. Add the marinated *papdi* and 1¼ cups of water. Cover and cook for 10 minutes or till the *papdi* gets cooked.
5. Drop spoonfuls of the dumpling batter into the *papdi* and cook on a high flame for 1 to 2 minutes so the dumplings are formed. Do not stir.

6. Cover and simmer for 5 to 7 minutes till the dumplings are cooked. Serve hot.

Nutritive values per serving

Energy	Protein	Carbohydrates	Invisible Fat	Fibre	Iron
76 cal	3.3 gm	14.4 gm	0.6 gm	0.5 gm	1.0 mg

Suva Moong Dal

The sweet taste of suva, mixed with moong dal and spiced with green chillies makes this subzi a must-try. Suva is rich in vitamin A and iron, while moong dal provides the necessary protein. So, what're you waiting for? Whip up and indulge in this lovely dish!

Preparation time: 15 minutes. Cooking time: 20 minutes. Serves 4.

½ cup yellow *moong dal* (split yellow gram)
½ tsp garlic paste
3 green chillies, slit
Salt to taste
1½ cups chopped dill leaves *(suva bhaji / shepu)*
1 tbsp freshly grated coconut for the garnish

1. Soak the *moong dal* for 30 minutes. Drain, wash and drain again. Keep aside.
2. Heat a non-stick *kadhai* on a medium flame and when hot, add the garlic paste, green chillies and *moong dal* and sauté for few minutes.
3. Lower the flame, add ¾ cup of water and salt and cook for 5 minutes or till the *moong dal* is tender but still firm.

4. Add the dill leaves, stir well and cover with a lid. Cook for 5 minutes.
5. Remove the lid and cook for few more minutes so all the water dries. Serve hot garnished with coconut.

Variation: SUVA CHANA DAL

Just substitute the yellow *moong dal* with *chana dal* (split Bengal gram) in this recipe.

Nutritive values per serving

Energy	Protein	Carbohydrates	Invisible Fat	Fibre	Vitamin A	Iron
81 cal	5.0 gm	12.1 gm	1.4 gm	0.3 gm	548.0 mcg	2.1 mg

Chole

As if it's not enough, that the traditional chole recipe is usually cooked with loads of oil, it is also served with calorie-laded puris! Here's is a healthy zero oil variation without unnecessary calories. When served with one meal of your day is thankfully guilt-free.

Preparation time: 10 minutes. Cooking time: 5 minutes. Serves 4.

¾ cup boiled potato cubes
2 tsp green chilli paste
1½ tsp garlic paste
2 tsp ginger, cut into thin strips
2 tsp *chana masala*
2 cups soaked and boiled *kabuli chana* (chick peas)
1 cup chopped tomatoes
1 tsp black salt (*sanchal*)
½ tsp dry mango powder (*amchur*)
Salt to taste
¼ cup chopped coriander (*dhania*) for the garnish

1. Heat a non-stick pan on a medium flame and when hot, add the potatoes and dry roast them for a few minutes on all sides till golden brown. Remove and drain on absorbent paper. Keep aside
2. Heat the non-stick pan again, add the green chilli paste, garlic paste and ginger and dry roast for about 30 seconds while stirring continuously. If the mixture starts burning sprinkle little water over it.
3. Add the *chana masala, kabuli chana*, potatoes, tomatoes, black salt, dry mango powder, salt and ½ cup of water and cook for 7 to 8 minutes.

   Serve hot garnished with coriander.

Nutritive values per serving

Energy	Protein	Carbohydrates	Invisible Fat	Fibre	Folic Acid	Sodium
115 cal	5.0 gm	20.6 gm	1.4 gm	1.4 gm	61.1 mcg	7.8 mg

Grated Cauliflower with Peas

Cauliflower is undoubtedly pleasing to the palate, in any, avatar! Calcium rich curds and milk powder add extra zing to this subzi, raising it to my favourites' list! Green peas are fibre-rich, thereby providing bulk and helping to get rid of the excess fat from the body a real boon to those who are trying to lose weight.

Preparation time: 10 minutes. Cooking time: 20 minutes. Serves 4.

½ tsp cumin seeds (*jeera*)
½ tsp coriander (*dhania*) powder
½ tsp turmeric power (*haldi*)
¼ cup sliced onions
1½ tsp grated ginger
½ tsp finely chopped green chillies
2 cups grated cauliflower
1 cup fresh green peas, boiled
1/3 cup blanched and chopped tomatoes
Salt to taste
2 tbsp low fat curds (*dahi*), page 100
1 tbsp milk powder

SOYA TUR DAL ROTI : Recipe on page 81. →

¼ tsp *garam masala*
1 tbsp chopped coriander (*dhania*) leaves for the garnish

1. Heat a non-stick *kadhai* on a medium flame and when hot, add the cumin seeds and dry roast for 10 seconds.
2. Add the coriander powder and turmeric powder and dry roast for another 2 seconds. Sprinkle a little water if the mixture starts burning.
3. Lower the flame, add the onions, ginger, green chillies and 2 to 3 tbsp water and cook while stirring continuously till the water evaporates.
4. Add the cauliflower, peas, tomatoes and salt. Cover and cook till the vegetables are tender.
5. Meanwhile, combine the curds, milk powder, *garam masala* and salt in a small bowl and whisk till smooth.
6. Add this curds mixture to the vegetables and cook for 4 to 5 minutes.
   Serve hot garnished with coriander.

Nutritive values per serving

Energy	Protein	Carbohydrates	Invisible Fat	Fibre	Calcium
63 cal	4.6 gm	9.6 gm	0.7 gm	2.1 gm	55.1 mg

Pumpkin Dry Vegetable

The health benefits of pumpkin are not too widely known, but it contains a horde of valuable nutrients like fibre, iron, folic acid, potassium, vitamin A and C. Soak in the health benefits of pumpkin, even as you delight in this delicious subzi, with steamed rice.

Preparation time: 10 minutes. Cooking time: 15 minutes. Serves 3.

¼ tsp fenugreek *(methi)* seeds
¼ tsp mustard seeds *(rai /sarson)*
¼ tsp cumin seeds *(jeera)*
¼ tsp fennel seeds *(saunf)*
½ tsp coriander *(dhania)* powder
½ tsp chilli powder
¼ cup sliced onions
1 tsp grated ginger
4 cups red pumpkin cubes
1 tsp sugar
Salt to taste
½ tsp turmeric powder *(haldi)*

½ tsp dry mango powder (*amchur*)

1. Heat a non-stick *kadhai* on a medium flame and when hot, add the fenugreek and mustard seeds and dry roast for 10 seconds.
2. Add the cumin seeds, fennel seeds, coriander powder and chilli powder. Sprinkle 2 tsp of water and cook while stirring continuously for few minutes.
3. Add the onions and ginger, and cook while stirring continuously till the onions turn golden brown.
4. Increase the flame, add the red pumpkin, sugar, salt, turmeric powder and ½ cup of water and cook till the water starts boiling.
5. Reduce the flame, cover with a lid and cook, stirring occasionally, till the pumpkin becomes tender.
6. Open the lid, add the dry mango powder and stir well.
7. Cook for 1 to 2 minutes and serve hot.

Nutritive values per serving

Energy	Protein	Carbohydrates	Invisible Fat	Fibre	Potassium
38 cal	1.8 gm	7.5 gm	0.1 gm	0.9 gm	179.9 mg

Gajar Fansi

Carrot, a storehouse of vitamin A, combines beautifully with French beans in this simple subzi. Peanuts are used in minor quantities to not only add crunch but also vitamin B3 to this subzi, making it delectable and nutritious.

Preparation time: 10 minutes. Cooking time: 15 minutes. Serves 4.

1 tsp cumin seeds (*jeera*)
½ cup chopped onions
1 tsp chilli powder
½ tsp turmeric powder (*haldi*)
½ tsp *garam masala*
2 cups chopped French beans (*fansi*)
1 cup chopped carrot
Salt to taste
2 tbsp roasted and coarsely crushed peanuts

1. Heat a non-stick *kadhai* on a medium flame and when hot, add the cumin seeds and onions and dry roast till the onions turn golden brown.

2. Lower the flame, add the chilli powder, turmeric powder, *garam masala* and cook while stirring continuously for 1 minute. Sprinkle a little water if the *masalas* start burning.
3. Add the French beans, carrot, ½ cup of water and salt, close the lid and cook till the vegetables are tender.
4. Add the peanuts, mix well and continue cooking for 2 more minutes.
   Serve hot.

Nutritive values per serving

Energy	Protein	Carbohydrates	Invisible Fat	Fibre	Vitamin A	Vitamin B_3
64 cal	2.7 gm	7.6 gm	2.5 gm	1.4 gm	422.6 mcg	1.3 mg

Soya Tur Dal Roti

Picture on page 75.

A healthy combination of 3 flours with tur dal makes this a real star recipe! Tur dal not only enhances the flavour but also adds vitamin B complex to these rotis. Garlic adds its unique flavour making these rotis a real pleasure to the connoisseur's taste buds.

Preparation time: 10 minutes. Cooking time: 30 minutes. Makes 6 *rotis*.

¼ cup soya flour
¼ cup cooked *tur* (arhar) *dal*
¼ cup *jowar* (white millet) flour
¼ cup whole wheat flour *(gehun ka atta)*
¼ tsp turmeric powder *(haldi)*
1½ tsp finely chopped coriander (*dhania*)
¼ tsp chilli powder
1 tsp coriander *(dhania)* powder
¼ tsp garlic paste
Salt to taste

Other ingredients
Whole wheat flour *(gehun ka atta)* for rolling

1. Combine all the ingredients in a bowl and knead into soft, smooth dough, using enough water.
2. Divide the dough into 6 equal portions.
3. Roll out again into a circle of 125 mm. (5") diameter, using whole wheat flour.
4. Place the *roti* on a non-stick *tava* (griddle). Turn over in a few seconds.
5. Cook the other side for a few more seconds.
6. Lift the *roti* with a pair of flat tongs and roast over an open flame till brown spots appear on both the sides.
7. Repeat with the remaining portions to make 5 more *rotis.*
   Serve hot.

Nutritive values per *roti*

Energy	Protein	Carbohydrates	Invisible Fat	Fibre	Vitamin B_1	Vitamin B_3
54 cal	3.0 gm	8.7 gm	0.8 gm	0.3 gm	0.1 mg	0.5 mg

Suva Chawal Roti

Picture on page 85.

Here's a variation of appas (rice bread) using suva bhaji, which not only has a pleasing sweetness but also a good store of vitamin A. Knead the dough when hot or else it will not be very smooth. It is best served with a spicy vegetable like Lauki Kofta Curry, page 15, because the paratha itself has a very mild, simple taste.

Preparation time: 10 minutes. Cooking time: 15 minutes. Makes 4 *rotis*.

½ cup chopped dill leaves *(shepu / suva bhaji)*
1½ cups rice flour (*chawal ka atta*)
1 tbsp finely chopped green chillies
Salt to taste

1. Combine the dill and rice flour and mix well. Keep aside.
2. Put 1 cup of water to boil in a thick-bottom pan and add the green chillies and salt.
3. Add the rice flour and stir for a minute.
4. Cover it with a lid and leave aside for about 5 minutes.
5. Knead into soft dough with a little water if required.
6. Divide the dough into 4 equal portions.

7. Roll out into a circle of 125 mm. (5") diameter, using rice flour.
8. Place the *roti* on a non-stick pan. Turn over in a few seconds.
9. Cook the other side for a few more seconds.
10. Lift the *roti* with a pair of flat tongs and roast over an open flame till brown spots appear on both the sides.
11. Repeat with the remaining portions to make 3 more *rotis.*
    Serve hot.

Nutritive values per *roti*

Energy	Protein	Carbohydrates	Invisible Fat	Fibre	Vitamin A
156 cal	3.1 gm	35.3 gm	0.2 gm	0.6 gm	179.6 mcg

SUVA CHAWAL ROTI : Recipe on page 83. →

Cauliflower Roti

Picture on page 37.

Don't settle for bland bajra rotis! Feast on these delicious cauliflower rotis instead. The grated garlic and spring onions really rev up the flavour of these rotis. Ensure that you roll the rotis immediately once the dough is kneaded, else it may turn soft and pose a problem while rolling. These rotis are cooked on direct flame to avoid the use of oil and make them crisp.

Preparation time: 10 minutes.   Cooking time: 30 minutes.   Makes 6 *rotis*.

¾ cup grated cauliflower
½ cup *bajra* (black millet) flour
1½ tbsp finely chopped spring onion whites
1½ tbsp finely chopped spring onion greens
2 tbsp finely chopped coriander (*dhania*)
½ tsp ginger-green chilli paste
½ tsp grated garlic
Salt to taste

Other ingredients
Bajra (black millet) flour for rolling

1. Combine all the ingredients and knead into a soft-smooth dough, using enough water.
2. Divide the dough into 6 equal portions.
3. Roll out one portion of the dough into a circle of 125 mm. (5") diameter.
4. Place the *roti* on the non-stick *tava* (griddle). Turn over in a few seconds.
5. Cook the other side for a few more seconds.
6. Lift the *roti* with a pair of flat tongs and roast on over an open flame till brown spots appear on both the sides.
7. Repeat with the remaining portions to make 5 more *rotis*.

Serve hot.

Nutritive values per *roti*

Energy	Protein	Carbohydrates	Invisible Fat	Fibre	Vitamin C
33 cal	1.2 gm	6.1 gm	0.4 gm	0.2 gm	6.6 mg

Ragi Roti

Taste bhi, health bhi! Really! Nutritious ragi flour is rich in iron, calcium and protein. Protein is required for the formation of new red blood cells and for building up your haemoglobin stores. Have these parathas to keep anemia at bay.

Preparation time: 10 minutes. Cooking time: 25 minutes. Makes 4 *rotis*.

½ cup *ragi / nachni* flour (red millet flour)
1½ tbsp finely chopped spring onion whites
1½ tbsp finely chopped spring onion greens
¼ cup grated carrots
1½ tbsp low fat curds *(dahi)*, page 100
½ tsp green chilli paste
Salt to taste

Other ingredients
Ragi / nachni flour (red millet flour) for rolling

1. Combine all the ingredients in a bowl and knead into soft-smooth dough, using enough water.
2. Divide the dough into 4 equal portions.
3. Roll out again into a circle of 125 mm. (5") diameter, using whole wheat flour.
4. Place the roti on a non-stick pan. Turn over in a few seconds.
5. Cook the other side for a few more seconds.
6. Lift the *roti* with a pair of flat tongs and roast over an open flame till brown spots appear on both the sides.
7. Repeat with the remaining portions to make 3 more *rotis*.

   Serve hot.

Nutritive values per *roti*

Energy	Protein	Carbohydrates	Invisible Fat	Fibre	Iron	Calcium
52 cal	1.4 gm	11.3 gm	0.2 gm	0.5 gm	0.7 mg	64.3 mg

Mooli Roti

Picture on back cover.

A popular breakfast option in most North Indian houses, theses parathas go well with a lot of subzis too. Here is an innovative version made with jowar flour and mashed potatoes, which help to make them soft.

Preparation time: 10 minutes. Cooking time: 30 minutes. Makes 5 *rotis*.

½ cup grated white radish *(mooli)*
½ cup *jowar* (white millet) flour
½ cup boiled, peeled and mashed potatoes
1 tbsp roasted coriander *(dhania)* seeds, lightly crushed
½ tsp chilli powder
¼ tsp turmeric powder *(haldi)*
¼ tsp dry mango powder (*amchur*)
Salt to taste

Other ingredients
Jowar (white millet) flour for rolling

1. Combine all the ingredients in a bowl and knead into a soft, smooth dough, using enough water.
2. Divide the dough into 5 equal portions.
3. Roll out one portion of the dough into a circle of 100 mm (4") diameter.
4. Place the *roti* on a non-stick *tava* (griddle). Turn over in a few seconds.
5. Cook the other side for a few more seconds.
6. Lift the *roti* with a pair of flat tongs and roast over an open flame till brown spots appear on both the sides.
7. Repeat with the remaining portions to make 4 more *rotis*.

   Serve hot.

Nutritive values per *roti*

Energy	Protein	Carbohydrates	Invisible Fat	Fibre	Iron
49 cal	1.3 gm	10.6 gm	0.2 gm	0.3 gm	0.5 mg

Besan Paratha

Picture on page 2.

Looking for something to serve with hot Tinda Masala, page 51? Try these tasty parathas, stuffed with roasted besan and simple yet tasty spices like green chillies. Whole wheat flour is a healthy option over refined flour as it is rich in fibre, iron and vitamin B complex.

Preparation time: 20 minutes. Cooking time: 30 minutes. Makes 5 *parathas*.

For the dough
1 cup whole wheat flour *(gehun ka atta)*
1½ tsp low fat curds (*dahi*), page 100
Salt to taste

To be mixed into a stuffing
½ cup roasted *besan* (Bengal gram flour)
1 tsp ginger-green chilli paste
¼ cup finely chopped coriander (*dhania*)
Salt to taste

Other ingredients
Whole wheat flour *(gehun ka atta)* for rolling

For the dough

1. Combine all the ingredients in a bowl and knead into a soft, smooth dough using water only if required.
2. Divide the dough into 5 equal portions. Keep aside.

How to proceed

1. Divide the stuffing into 5 equal portions. Keep aside.
2. Roll one portion of the dough into a circle of 75 mm. (5") diameter.
3. Spread one portion of the stuffing in an even layer on the circle and roll into a cigar-shape.
4. Press and roll again into a spiral like a *chakli.*
5. Roll out again into a circle of 125 mm. (5") diameter, using whole wheat flour.
6. Cook on a hot non-stick *tava* (griddle), until both sides are golden brown.
7. Lift the *paratha* with a pair of flat tongs and roast over an open flame till brown spots appear on both the sides.
8. Repeat with the remaining dough and the stuffing to make 4 more *parathas.* Serve hot.

Nutritive values per *paratha*

Energy	Protein	Carbohydrates	Invisible Fat	Fibre	Iron
105 cal	4.4 gm	20.0 gm	0.8 gm	0.5 gm	1.5 mg

Tandoori Paratha

The well-thought-out choice of spices in the stuffing is sure to delight your taste buds. This healthy variation of Tandoori Paratha is a sure hit! Oil is usually added to the flour to make a smooth and soft dough, but to curb the use of oil, I have added low fat curds which also produces the desired effect.

Preparation time: 20 minutes. Cooking time: 25 minutes. Makes 4 *parathas*.

For the dough
1 cup whole wheat flour (*gehun ka atta*)
1½ tsp low fat curds (*dahi*), page 100
Salt to taste

For the stuffing
½ cup grated cauliflower
½ cup grated French beans (*fansi*)
½ cup grated capsicum
½ cup thick low fat curds (*dahi*), page 100
1 tsp *tandoori masala*
1 tsp garlic paste

1 tsp ginger-green chilli paste
2 tsp red chilli paste
1 tsp *besan (*Bengal gram flour)
Salt to taste

Other ingredients
Whole wheat flour *(gehun ka atta)* for rolling

For the dough
1. Combine all the ingredients in a bowl and knead into a soft-smooth dough, using water only if required.
2. Divide the dough into 4 equal portions. Keep aside.

For the stuffing
1. Combine all the ingredients in a bowl and mix well.
2. Heat a non-stick *tava* (griddle), add the mixture and sauté for 5 minutes or till all the water evaporates.
3. Cool and divide the stuffing into 4 equal portions. Keep aside.

How to proceed
1. Roll out one portion of the dough into a circle of 75 mm. (3") diameter.

2. Place one portion of the stuffing mixture in the centre of the circle.
3. Bring together all the sides in the centre and seal tightly.
4. Roll out again into a circle of 125 mm. (5") diameter, using whole wheat flour.
5. Place the *paratha* on a non-stick *tava* (griddle) pan. Turn over in a few seconds.
6. Cook the other side for a few more seconds.
7. Lift the *paratha* with a pair of flat tongs and roast over an open flame till brown spots appear on both the sides.
8. Repeat with the remaining portions to make 3 more *parathas*.
   Serve hot.

Nutritive values per *paratha*

Energy	Protein	Carbohydrates	Invisible Fat	Fibre	Calcium
109 cal	4.6 gm	21.5 gm	0.6 gm	1.0 gm	45.6 mg

Masala Paratha

Picture on cover.

This recipe is sure to tempt you to come back for another serving! Whether served as it is or with a vegetable, this is definitely a delicacy. Mashed potatoes and low fat curds make these parathas soft and delicious, while soya flour increases its nutritive value by adding protein, iron and zinc.

Preparation time: 20 minutes. Cooking time: 25 minutes. Makes 4 *parathas*.

For the dough

¾ cup whole wheat flour *(gehun ka atta)*
¼ cup soya flour
¼ cup boiled and mashed potatoes
1½ tbsp low fat curds *(dahi)*, page 100
Salt to taste

To be mixed into a stuffing

2 tbsp roasted fennel seeds *(saunf)*, lightly crushed
2 tsp chilli flakes
½ roasted onion, page 11, roughly chopped

2 tbsp coriander *(dhania)* powder, lightly crushed
2 tsp dry mango powder (*amchur*)
Salt to taste

Other ingredients
Whole wheat flour *(gehun ka atta)* for rolling

For the dough

1. Combine all the ingredients in a bowl and knead into soft dough using enough water.
2. Divide the dough into 4 equal portions. Keep aside.

How to proceed

1. Roll out one portion of the dough into a circle of 75 mm. (3") diameter.
2. Place one portion of the stuffing mixture in the centre of the circle.
3. Bring together all the sides in the centre and seal tightly.
4. Roll out again into a circle of 150 mm. (6") diameter, using whole wheat flour.
5. Place the *paratha* on a non-stick pan. Turn over in a few seconds.
6. Cook the other side for a few more seconds.
7. Lift the *paratha* with a pair of flat tongs and roast over an open flame till brown spots appear on both the sides.

8. Repeat with the remaining portions to make 3 more *parathas*.
   Serve hot.

Nutritive values per *paratha*

Energy	Protein	Carbohydrates	Invisible Fat	Fibre	Iron	Zinc
102 cal	4.7 gm	18.1 gm	1.2 gm	0.6 gm	1.5 mg	0.9 mg

Low Fat Curds

Made from low fat milk (99.9% fat free) locally available in the market. These curds provides only 71 calories and 0.2 gm. fat per cup. It tastes same like full fat curds.

Preparation time: 5 minutes. Setting time: 5 to 6 hours. Makes 5 cups.

1 litre low fat milk (readily available in the market)
1 tbsp curds

1. Warm the milk.
2. Add the curds, mix well and cover.
3. Keep aside until the curds set (approx. 5 to 6 hours).
4. During the cold climate, place inside a casserole or closed oven to set.

Nutritive values per cup

Energy	Protein	Carbohydrates	Invisible Fat	Fibre
75 cal	7.1 gm	10.4 gm	0.2 gm	0 gm

Low Fat Paneer

Paneer is usually high in fat, but we have made it low calorie by using low fat milk and low fat curds. Using curds instead of lemon juice not only gives more amount of paneer comparatively but also renders it soft. Use freshly made paneer to get better results as it gets blended well and gives body and creamy texture to any recipe.

Preparation time: 20 minutes. Setting time: 10 minutes. Makes 70 grams (approx. ½ cup).

3 cups low fat milk
1½ cups low fat curds (*dahi*), page 100, beaten

1. Put the milk to boil in a broad pan. When it starts boiling, add the curds and mix well.
2. Remove from the heat and stir gently until the milk curdles.
3. Strain and tie the curdled milk in a muslin cloth. Hang for about half an hour to allow the whey to drain out.
4. Use as required.

Nutritive values per ½ cup

Energy	Protein	Carbohydrates	Invisible Fat	Fibre
315 cal	31.5 gm	45.0 gm	0.2 gm	0.0 gm

Vegetable Stock

Use this vegetable stock instead of water, as in the recipe of Khatta Gobhi, page 21, Mushroom and Green Peas Curry, page 36, etc. for an additional flavourful touch these gravies.

Preparation time: 5 minutes. Setting time: 20 minutes. Makes 4½ cups.

½ cup roughly chopped cabbage
½ cup roughly chopped carrots
¼ cup chopped celery
2 tbsp chopped spring onions
3 to 4 cauliflower florets
3-4 cloves (*laung / lavang*)
25 mm (1") stick cinnamon (*dalchini*)
1 bayleaf (*tejpatta*)
Salt to taste

1. Boil all the ingredients in 6 cups of water on a medium flame for 15 to 20 minutes, till it reduces to about 4½ cups.
2. Allow the vegetables to settle at the bottom of the vessel and drain out the stock. Discard the vegetables.
   Use the stock as required.

A magazine by **TARLA DALAL**

Book your copy now...

Price : Rs. 50/-

Available at your nearest bookstore, newspaper stands and tarladalal.com

SUBSCRIBE NOW & Get Free Bonus Membership at tarladalal.com

Pick any one of the subscription offers and send us a cheque or a Demand Draft in favour of "Sanjay & Co." along with your detailed address including pin code, telephone no. and e-mail address.

Addressed to :
Sanjay & Co. 353, A-1, Shah & Nahar Industrial Estate,
Dhanraj Mill Compound, Lower Parel (W),
Mumbai 400013. INDIA

5 years (30 issues) + 1 Year Free Membership = Rs. 1450/-*

3 Years (18 issues) + 9 Months Free Membership = Rs. 1080/-*

1 Year (6 issues) + 2 Months Free Membership = Rs. 340/-*

***Offer valid for shipments only within India and is inclusive of shipping & handling charges.**

For overseas shipments log on to tarladalal.com
For more information, call us on our helpline no. (022) 2496 8068 on all weekdays between 9.30 a.m. and 4.30 p.m. or write to us at subscription@tarladalal.com

Total Health Series

TARLA DALAL
INDIA'S # 1 COOKERY AUTHOR
COOKBOOKS

Healthy Diabetic Cooking

Exotic Diabetic Cooking
Part - 1

Growing Kids Cook Book

Soya Rotis & Subzis

Healthy Heart Cookbook

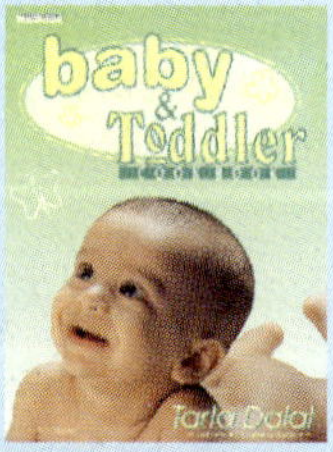

Baby & Toddler Cook Book

Cooking with
1 Teaspoon of Oil

Low Calorie
Healthy Cooking

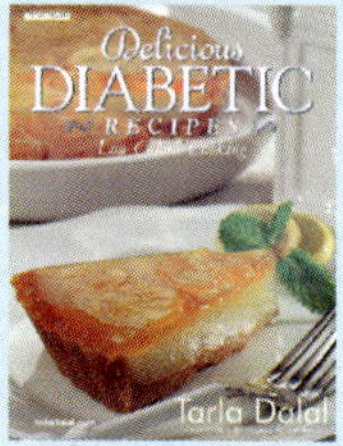

Delicious Diabetic Recipes

Pregnancy Cook Book